Popular Christmas Memories

MELODY BOBER

7 Late Intermediate Piano Arrangements of the Season's Most Popular Songs

When I think of Christmas, I am reminded of so many happy memories. These include a visit to grandma's, an extremely tall and beautiful Christmas tree, brightly wrapped presents, homemade goodies, and, of course, family sing-a-longs.

While sacred carols give the reason for the season, secular songs celebrate holiday delights such as a snow fall ("Winter Wonderland," "Let It Snow! Let It Snow! Let It Snow!"), a sleigh ride ("Sleigh Ride") or the magic of a first Christmas together ("It Must Have Been the Mistletoe"). A song can share the spirit of the season ("Have Yourself a Merry Little Christmas") or provide a more nostalgic reflection ("(There's No Place Like) Home for the Holidays"). And some songs are just plain fun ("It's the Most Wonderful Time of the Year")!

In *Popular Christmas Memories,* Book 3, I have arranged some of my favorite Christmas songs. It is my hope that your special Christmas memories will be rekindled during the holiday season through the pieces in this collection.

Merry Christmas!

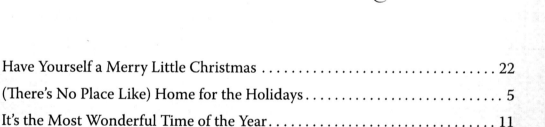

Alfred

Copyright © MMIX by Alfred Music Publishing Co., Inc.
All Rights Reserved   Printed in USA
ISBN-10: 0-7390-6394-4
ISBN-13: 978-0-7390-6394-1

Winter Wonderland

Words by Dick Smith
Music by Felix Bernard
Arr. by Melody Bober

(There's No Place Like) Home for the Holidays

Words by Al Stillman
Music by Robert Allen
Arr. by Melody Bober

Let It Snow! Let It Snow! Let It Snow!

Words by Sammy Cahn
Music by Jule Styne
Arr. by Melody Bober

It's the Most Wonderful Time of the Year

Words and Music by Eddie Pola and George Wyle
Arr. by Melody Bober

It Must Have Been the Mistletoe

Words and Music by Justin Wilde and Doug Konecky
Arr. by Melody Bober

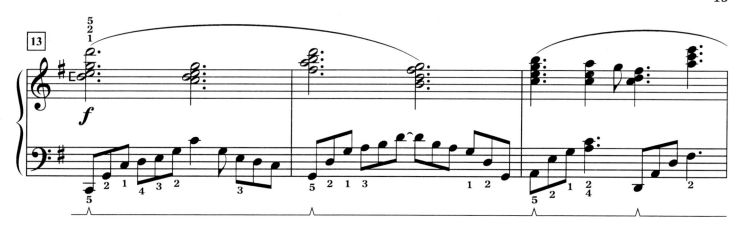

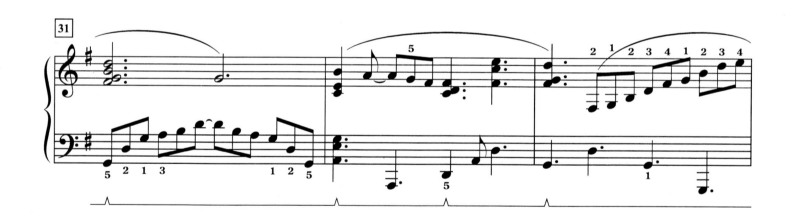

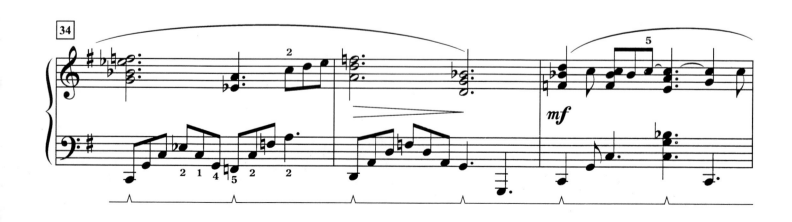

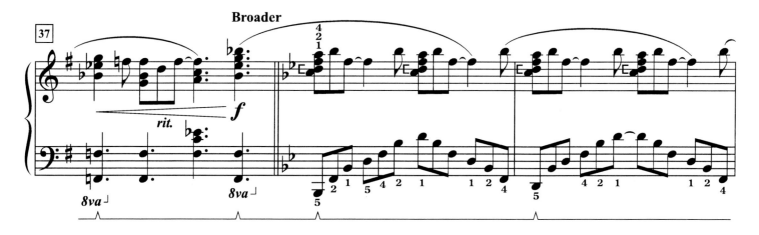

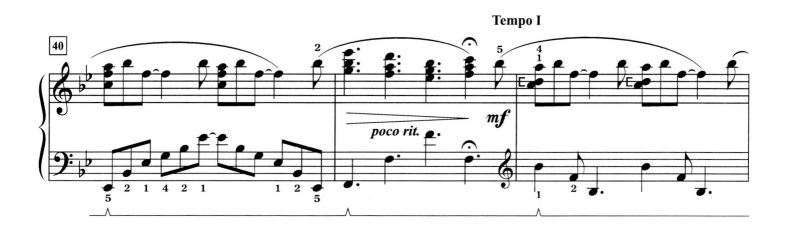

Sleigh Ride

Music by Leroy Anderson
Words by Mitchell Parish
Arr. by Melody Bober

Have Yourself a Merry Little Christmas

Words and Music by Hugh Martin and Ralph Blane
Arr. by Melody Bober